# Look at Wool

Written by **Alison Milford**

# Fast phonics

Before reading this book, ask the student to practise saying the sounds (phonemes) and reading the new words used in the book. Try to make it as speedy and as fun as possible.

## Read the tricky high frequency words

The student can't sound out these words at the moment, but they need to know them because they are commonly used.

| for | all | do | they | the | I | onto |
| --- | --- | --- | --- | --- | --- | --- |
| no | my | be | so | of | we | are |

**Tip:** Encourage the student to sound out any sounds they know in these words, and you can provide them with the irregular or tricky part.

## Say the sounds

long oo    short oo

ai    ee    igh    oa    ar

The 'oo' grapheme can make two different sounds (the 'oo' in 'book' makes a shorter sound than the 'oo' in 'spoon'). Talk to the student about this difference and point it out in words as you come across the grapheme in this book.

**Tip:** Remember to say the pure sounds. For example, 'sssss' and 'nnnnn'. If you need a reminder, watch the *Snappy Sounds* videos.

## Snappy words

Point at a word randomly and have the student read the word. The student will need to sound out the word and blend the sounds to read the word. For example: 'b–oo–t–sss, boots'.

| wool | too  | broom |
| look | cool | spool |
| good | food |       |
| wood | loom |       |
| hood | boots |      |
| hook | loops |      |

## Quick vocabulary check

The underlined words may not be familiar to the student. Check their understanding before you start to read the book.

We can get wool from sheep and goats.

We can get wool from alpacas, too!

Dad cuts the wool off the sheep. It gets a good trim.

They look cool with no wool.

I sweep up the thick wool with my broom.

The wool feels soft.

Next, Nan twists and turns it onto a wood spool.

We can stain the wool.
It will be red and green
and black.

Look. This wool will be red.

wool

loops of wool

The wool is wet so we hang it up.

wool food

When the wool is set, we can do lots of things with it.

Lots of fun things are wool.

Look at the rug on the loom.

Dad can go in with the wool and then back again, too.

bright wool boots

We can hook the wool.

We did wool boots for all the children.

Dad and Nan did a wool hat and a hood, too.

Wool pom-poms are fun to do, too.

This pom-pom is from my red wool.

# Comprehension questions

Well done!

### Let's talk about the story together

Ask the student:
- What did you learn about in this book?
- What animals can we get wool from?
- What is a loom?
- Why is wool important to us? What do you have that is made of wool?

### Snappy words

Ask the student to read these words as quickly as they can.

| wool | look | food | too |
| cool | good | boots | loops |

### Fluency

Can the student read the story again and improve on the last time?

**Have fun!**